THE WOMAN'S WORLD OF GOLF

by

Joseph Quinzi and Catherine McKenzie Shane

Art By: *Susan Moore*

Photography By: *Aneta W. Sperber*

1980 Copyright © by Joseph Quinzi and Catherine Shane
All Rights Reserved
Printed in the United States of America

ISBN 0-89917-300-4

Reproduced by photo offset from typeset manuscript.
For information, write T.I.S. Publications Division, P.O. Box 1998,
Bloomington, Indiana 47402.

PREFACE

Golf is a uniquely personal game. It is a game of muscle movement and body coordination--the movement of *your* muscles and *your* body as they move rhythmically through the ball. This book will provide you with guidelines for building your *own* golf swing. We do not ask, nor even want you, to copy any one else's golf swing. What we hope is that you will make golf *your* game by adapting proven techniques and principles to your own muscle build and physique. While the techniques demonstrated within this book are particularly suited to women, they have worked equally well for men. There is no reason, therefore, why men cannot benefit from reading--and putting into practice!--the principles enumerated in this book.

There is an old Scottish saying we would like to share with all of you.

"It's no' what ye hae, but what ye dae wi' what ye hae, that coonts."
(It's not what you have, but what you do with what you have, that counts.)

Whether you are tall or small, fat or lean, seven or seventy, this book is dedicated to you, the women golfers, members of that unique sorority of sportswomen who live in *The Woman's World of Golf.*

THE WOMAN'S WORLD OF GOLF

Foreword by Betsy Rawls, Tour Director, L.P.G.A.

Few people realize that women's participation in golf dates back far beyond the 20th century. If the history books are correct, the first woman golfer on record was Mary Queen of Scotts who, as legend goes, preferred to play "golfe" with her "cadet" (caddy) on the grounds of Seton Castle rather than mourn the death of her recently departed husband, The Earl of Bothwell. Queen Mary probably rates, then, as the first "golf widow" in the history of golf!

Women's golf in the United States, however, didn't get off to a start until the turn of this century when, in 1896, women were first permitted to play on their own nine-hole course at Shinnecock Hills Club on Long Island. From that time on, women's participation in golf has been on the ascendency, first at the amateur level and later, on the professional tour. The early years of women's golf are star-studded with such personalities as the Curtiss Sisters (for whom the Curtiss Cup is named), Louise Suggs, Patty Berg, Beth Jameson, Joyce Wethered of Great Britain, and the fabled "Babe" Zaharias.

With the founding of the L.P.G.A. in 1950, women's golf gained added dimension, as outstanding professional women golfers participated in tournaments across the country. In these beginning days of pro golf, prize money was very small, with the average purse running between $3,500 and $5,000--in total! This helps to explain why the first tournaments attracted relatively few women pros. Today, however, with fields running on the average of one hundred players, and with well over two million dollars recently being offered in prize money, it's easy to see why competition and the enthusiasm of the participants have increased enormously. As a result, players must produce increasingly high standards of performance--much to the delight of the ever-growing gallery of fans who find women's professional golf just as fascinating, exciting, and even more attractive to follow than the men's tour.

The woman's world of golf is a many-faceted one, for amateurs and professionals alike. It's a world of thought and action, of suspense and drama, of fun and frustration, of heartbreaking defeat and superb achievement. It's an ever-growing world which attracts increasing numbers of women, both young and old, who are intrigued by the challenge of this fascinating and most difficult sport. To meet that challenge and to overcome it--such is the joy and the reward for those of us who live in *The Woman's World of Golf.*

THE WOMAN'S WORLD OF GOLF

CHAPTER ONE

CHOOSING YOUR EQUIPMENT

The Golf Club

A golf club is made up of seven basic parts, the head comprising the toe, face, and heel.

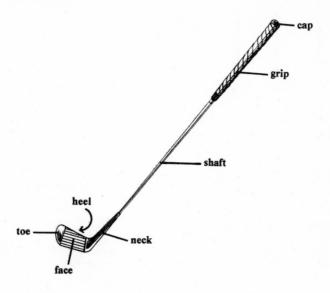

An average set of clubs for women consists of fourteen clubs. These include: seven irons, one pitching wedge, one sand wedge, one putter, and three woods.

The average weight of a woman's club is 12 to 13 ounces. Women's sets frequently do not contain the Number 2 iron since the distance variation between the Number 2 and 3 irons is slight. Only experienced golfers can use the 2 iron with maximum effectiveness. Occasionally, touring pros will use a Number 1 iron on the fairway. Since the Number 1 iron has a very closed face, it is difficult to use and is not recommended for the average golfer.

A Look At The Irons

There are ten irons in an average set of women's clubs. As the illustration shows, the loft or slant of the club face of each iron increases as the irons increase in number. As the loft increases, the length of the shaft decreases by approximately four inches. Thus, the Number 3 iron has the longest shaft and the least amount of loft. This enables the ball to travel long and low.

On the other hand, the Number 9 iron has greater loft and less shaft. This will cause the ball to travel high and short. A good rule of thumb for irons is: The further away from the green, the lower the club number. The closer to the green, the higher the club number.

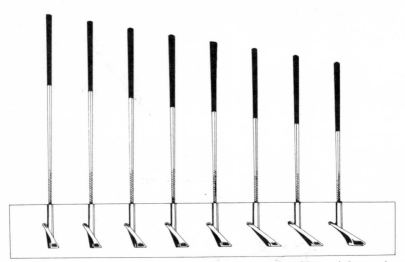

There are ten irons in an average set of women's clubs -- eight regular irons plus a sand wedge and occasionally a number two iron.

Irons For Traps And Rough

The *pitching wedge,* or Number 10 iron, is built to give you more weight and loft, which enables you to pitch the ball out of heavy grass or fairway turf.

The *sand wedge* differs from the pitching wedge because of the flange which runs from heel to toe.

The flange enables you to blast sand from a trap, giving the ball sufficient height and momentum to carry it high into the air and onto the putting surface.

Experienced women golfers sometimes use the sand wedge to lift the ball out of heavy, coarse grass, if the ball is embedded there. This, however, requires considerable skill and is not recommended for beginning golfers.

The putter has the least amount of loft of all the irons. There are many different styles of putters. The most popular are shown below.

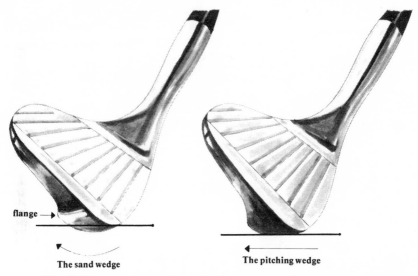

flange →

The sand wedge

The pitching wedge

The flange on the sand wedge helps blast the sand, together with the ball, from the trap.

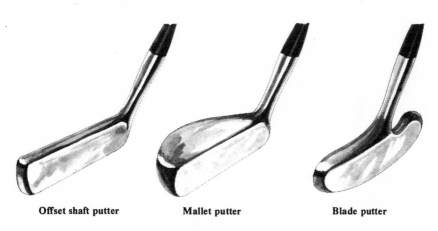

Offset shaft putter   Mallet putter   Blade putter

Putters also vary in weight and height. It is a good idea for beginners to get a professional's advice on the selection of the putter, as well as the other clubs in the set.

Distances For Irons

The distance a ball will travel varies considerably according to the ability and experience of the golfer. A top woman professional may hit a Number 3 iron as far as 180 yards.

The following chart gives yardage for the average woman golfer.

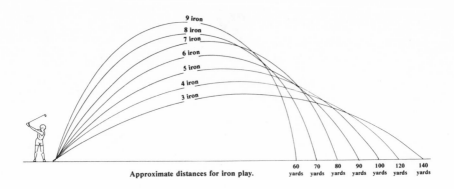

Approximate distances for iron play.

| 60 yards | 70 yards | 80 yards | 90 yards | 100 yards | 120 yards | 140 yards |

The Woods

A full set of woods consists of four clubs: The "driver," or Number 1 wood, and the Number 3, 4, and 5 woods. Usually, there is no Number 2 wood because of its closeness in appearance and function to the driver.

The driver or Number 1 wood, has the least amount of loft and the longest shaft of all the woods. It is the club with which you will most often use to tee off the teeing area.

The height of the tee will vary according to the preference of the player. Generally, one half of the ball should appear above the club head when you assume your position or *address* the ball.

Address position for driver. Ball should line up with inside of left heel.

The Numbers 3, 4, and 5 fairway woods are designed to give your ball maximum loft from the fairway, without benefit of a tee.

The fairway woods increase in loft but shorten in shaft length as they increase in number. As is the case with irons, we find that the lower the club number, the further the ball will travel. The higher the club number, the higher and shorter the ball will travel.

Many amateur and professional women golfers like to use the Number 5 wood off the fairway because of the relatively wide loft of the club face which enables the club to lift the ball high off the turf.

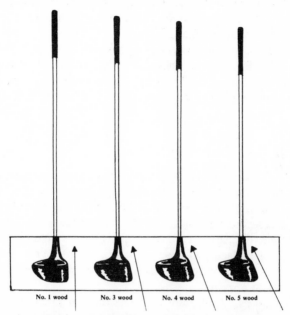

| No. 1 wood | No. 3 wood | No. 4 wood | No. 5 wood |

There are four woods in an average set of women's clubs.
Not illustrated is the No. 7 wood which is especially helpful for difficult shots out of the rough, as well as for par-3 holes.

Distances For Woods

Distances obtained from woods will vary according to the player. For example, touring woman professional, Mickey Wright, set the record for the longest drive with a tee shot of 280 yards. Most women touring pros will average from 210 to 240 yards off the tee.

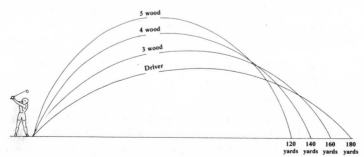

Approximate distances for woods.

A Note On Starter Sets

If you are just taking up golf, and are unwilling to invest in a full set of clubs, it is recommended that you purchase a "starter set." This comprises the Numbers 3, 5, 7, and 9 irons; one putter; one driver; and one Number 3 wood. A small, light canvas bag is the best choice when you carry this limited number of clubs.

Once you gain experience in golf, and learn how to obtain distance and height variation from a variety of clubs, you should then plan to purchase a complete set of clubs. Again, seek the advice of a professional for the club weight which is most suited to your height and build.

Your Golf Bag And Wardrobe

The Golf Bag. If you are an experienced golfer and have invested in a full set of clubs, it is advisable to purchase a large, spacious golf bag. Golf clubs should not be crowded together since this can harm club grips due to the friction and rubbing that results from space limitation. *A word about golf tubes:* Unless you are an "organization woman" who likes to have everything in place, golf tubes for each club are not recommended. They add unnecessary weight to the bag and do not protect club grips from friction and abrasion.

Head Covers. While they can be aesthetically pleasing, the basic function of head covers is to protect the heads of wooden clubs from bumping together and scratching during play. Some golfers, in the belief that it will save a few minutes, remove head covers at the beginning of play. This defeats the purpose of having covers and, at a time when they are most vulnerable, cause needless damage to woods through scratching.

The Golf Glove. There are four reasons why a golf glove should be worn during play:

1. It helps you grip the club firmly.

2. It protects the beginning player from getting blisters during practice sessions.

3. It protects the experienced player from developing an excess number of callouses during lengthy practice sessions.

4. It protects the player from excessive hand perspiration which could cause the hand to slip down on the club grip with consequent loss of control.

(It is not uncommon, by the way, for women pros on tour to go through two to three gloves during the course of one round of competition.) Short finger gloves, which cover the palm only, are not recommended since they give the fingers no protection. A few rounds of play will convince you that full finger gloves are more desirable.

Clothing. Many women like to wear hats or visors during play. This is a good idea. Hats not only give protection from the sun, they keep hair from blowing in the face, absorb excessive perspiration, and aid vision during play.

A loose-fitting blouse is important because it gives you maximum mobility while swinging the club. Culottes, skirts, shorts, and slacks are popular with women golfers, as are one-piece golf dresses. By all means, wear bright, flattering colors: Better to be a colorful moving target than a dull one -- especially at the nineteenth hole!

Shoes. The spiked golf shoe is essential to give you needed stability during the golf swing. Without the anchoring effect of spiked shoes, the golfer is more apt to slide or lose balance during her swing. When selecting shoes, remember that you will be wearing heavy, cotton socks on the course. Comfort is the keynote to the golf shoe, so don't let the shoe pinch.

A word to the beginning golfer:

If you are just taking up the game, and are unwilling to invest in expensive shoes, wear tennis shoes during practice sessions. Once you have decided to make golf your game, then go ahead and purchase a good pair of spiked shoes.

Jewelry. Touring women pros seldom if ever wear any kind of jewelry during play – watches and wedding bands in particular. The impact of the club head hitting the ball can damage a wrist watch, while rings can have an abrasive effect on the grip or create uncomfortable ring callouses.

CHAPTER TWO

YOUR GOLF GRIP AND STANCE

The Golf Grip

There are three basic, widely used golf grips. These are The *Baseball* Grip, The *Interlock* Grip, and The *Overlap* Grip.

The Baseball Grip

The simple baseball or "full finger" grip is often recommended for beginning golfers.

When preparing to grip the club, always place your feet together, stand up straight, and let your arms fall by your side. Place the club in a line between your feet and gently lean it against your right hand, as shown below.

Next, bring your left arm straight out from your side, fingers and thumb close together. Place your left hand on the club, about four inches from the top. Wrap four fingers around the shaft, and place your thumb down the center of the shaft. Once it is in position, your club will rest comfortably in the hollow of your thumb and fourth finger. The palm of your left hand should be facing in the same direction as the club face. Thus your left arm, hand and the club should form a straight line, with the club acting as an extension of your left arm and hand.

STAGES IN GRIPPING A CLUB

Stage I	Start with your feet together and concentrate on your hands! Gently lean the club against your right hand.
Stage II	Bring your left hand straight from your side, fingers and thumb close together.
Stage III	Place left hand on club about two inches from top.
Stage IV	Position thumb down center of shaft.
Stage V	Put slight pressure on first three fingertips of left hand.
Stage VI	Left arm, hand and club form straight line.

Stage VII   Place right hand on shaft covering thumb of left hand with hollow of right.

Stage VIII   Palms of both hands should face inward on shaft.

Stage I

Stage II

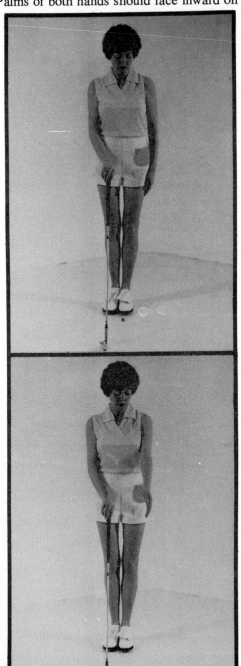

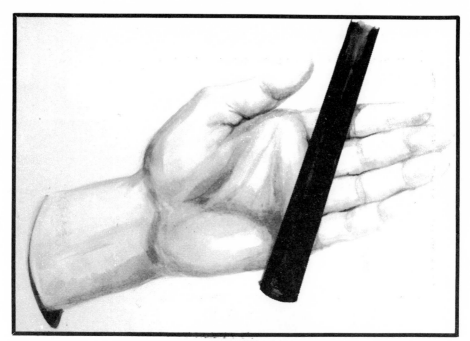

Stage III a.

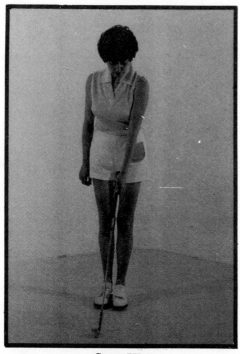

Stage III b.

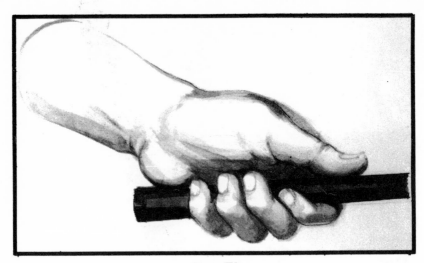

Stage IV

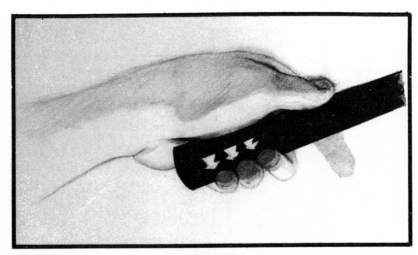

Stage V

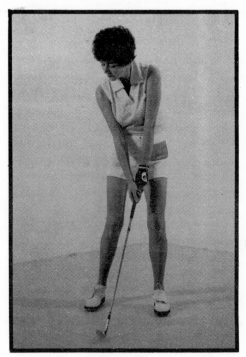

Stage VI

Stage VII

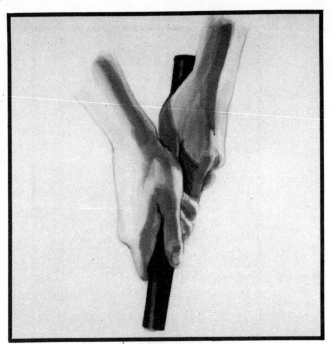

Stage VIII

While holding the club with your left hand, place your right hand on the shaft immediately below your left hand. Wrap the four fingers of your right hand around the club, keeping your thumb on top of the shaft, slightly to the left of center. Cover the thumb of your left hand with the hollow of your right hand. If you hold the club up, you should be able to see eight fingers in a row on the shaft, with the right thumb pointing down the shaft in an eleven o'clock position. The palms of both your hands should be facing inward on the shaft as shown in the illustration.

The Interlock Grip

Because it does not require large or muscular hands, the interlock grip is the most commonly used grip by professional and amateur women golfers. Many touring pros use the interlock grip because it places a natural pressure on the fingertips of the first three fingers of the left hand. This is extremely important, as we explain in the next section on hand pressure.

To form the interlock grip, place your left hand on the club as you did for the baseball grip. The left arm, hand and club should form a straight and unbroken line.

Next, bring your right hand toward the club with the palm facing the shaft. Place the little finger of your right hand in between the third and fourth fingers of your left hand, as shown below.

The Overlap or Varden Grip

The overlap grip was first developed by Harry Varden, one of Britain's golfing "greats" at the turn of the century. Because the grip requires strong hands and is the most unnatural of all the golf grips, it is seldom used by women and is not recommended for beginning golfers. To form the overlap grip, place the left hand on the shaft and bring the right hand over, covering the fourth finger of the left hand with your right little finger, as illustrated below.

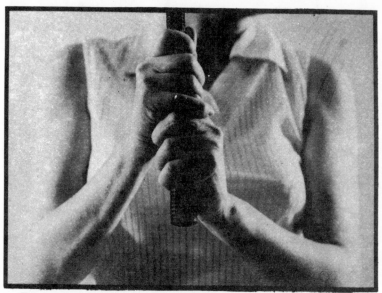

The overlap grip meshes left and right hand into one power unit.

Ideally, the overlap grip should cause the right and left hands to mesh together into one unit -- the desirable goal each golfer should strive to attain no matter which grip she selects.

Hand Pressure

Hand pressure is one of the most crucial parts of your golf game. Without proper hand pressure, the woman golfer is unable to develop her fullest potential. Furthermore, she is very likely to run into serious difficulties with all aspects of her golf game without correct hand pressure.

In the previous section, we discussed the importance of the left arm, the hand, and the club forming one, unbroken power unit. An essential part of that power comes from the pressure exerted on the tips of the first three fingers of the left hand. These three fingers not only control the line of the backswing; they bring power to the swing through the ball. Without constant left hand pressure, your game will lack consistency.

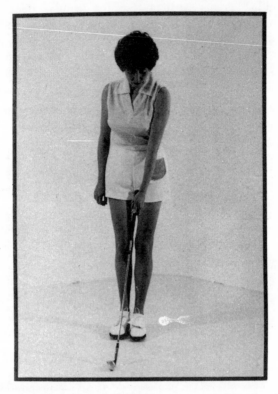

Left arm, left hand and club form one power unit with "power pressure" generated from first three fingers of left hand.

Here is a simple experiment which will help illustrate our point. Put your feet together, then place your left hand on the club. As you do so, exert pressure on your thumb and fourth finger. Next, take a backswing. You will note that the club head tends to roll away from the back of the hand, rather than stay in line with it. The club head and back of the hand should always move along the same line to ensure as little deviation as possible in the line of the club toward the target. Next, grip the club, placing pressure on the first three fingertips of your left hand. Gently, and with no pressure, place your fourth finger and thumb into position. Swing back in a straight line. This time, the club head and back of the hand will move along the same line, with both directed toward the target.

If the upper three fingers of the left hand are in control, what is the function of the right hand?

The primary role of the right hand in golf is to help you hold the club in a stable position at the start of the swing and to steady the club during the execution of the entire swing. There should be little or no pressure exerted by the right hand at any time during the swing. The right hand simply acts as a brace to the left, and should not dominate it. Many golfers, regardless of whether they are right or left handed, naturally want to bring their right arm and hand overly much into play. This causes numerous problems in their game, which we will discuss in the chapter, YOUR GOLF CLINIC: "Causes and Cures of Golfing Ailments."

Try to minimize the dominance of your right hand as much as possible. It will automatically get into play without your help! Once you feel confident that your left hand is in control, place a slight amount of pressure on the two, center fingers of your right hand. The pressure will enable you to exert maximum control as the club face moves through the ball. You should only do this, however, once you are sure that your left hand is in complete control throughout the swing.

The Stance

Always begin your golf stance with your feet together and with your club head centered in an imaginary line between your feet. Remember that your golf stance must start somewhere. *Always start it with your feet together.* Once your feet are positioned together, move your left foot one inch to the left and your right foot two inches to the right. Continue this movement until you have positioned the ball either to the center or slightly forward of center between your feet.

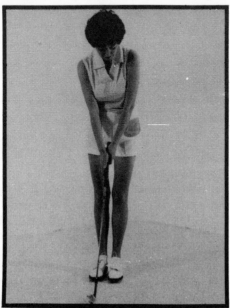

Always start your golf stance with feet together and with club head centered in an imaginary line between your feet.

While it may seem strange to move your feet inches at a time, your right foot moving twice as far as your left, the purpose is to avoid the natural tendency most golfers have to play the ball off their right side. Many golfers unknowingly play the ball off their right, mistakenly believing that they are, in fact, playing it off center. Touring pros are very much aware of this tendency. A close look at the top pros will show that they almost always begin their stance with feet together. Knowing that their left foot will naturally move too far to the left, the pros will purposely move their right foot twice as far as their left. This move ensures that the ball will be properly centered, ready for play.

Once you have centered the ball between your feet, line your feet with the target. (At this point, your club face, the back of your left hand and your feet should all be pointing in the same direction.)

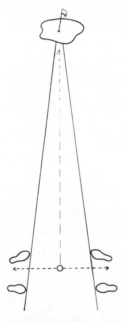

Whether you play right or left-handed golf, make sure that your feet and club are lined up to the target.

Next, move the toe of your left foot slightly outward at a 45 degree angle so that it is pointing a little to the left of your target. This position will enable you to swing more easily through the ball and avoid excess twisting or strain on the left ankle. It will also help you to roll or swivel your body through the ball at impact.

The right toe should remain straight, giving you a solid base during your back swing. It is important in the backswing that you brace yourself with your lower right side which supports the upper part of your body as it swivles around.

"Sitting" On The Ball

The feet are crucial to maintaining balance during your golf swing. Improper distribution of weight on your feet will cause lack of balance and subsequent loss of control and power during the swing.

In order to achieve proper balance, you must assume a slight "sitting" position while addressing the ball prior to play. To do this, stand upright, then imagine that you are about to sit on a chair. The "sitting" movement will cause a slight transfer of weight onto your heels, bringing the lower part of your body closer to the ground. Your club will automatically move slightly further out and away from your body. At this point, your left knee should be slightly bent forward. Never throw your left knee outward, since this will weaken your left side as you swing through the ball. Your right knee at address should incline toward your left knee.

Weight distribution at the beginning of the swing should be evenly spread from the ball of your foot to the back of your heel. At no time should your weight be on your toes, since this could bring about a "toppling over" effect during the swing and cause you to lose balance.

"Sitting" on the ball gives you a solid base for balance throughout the entire swing.

Finding Your Natural Club Position

The following simple exercise will help you find the club position best suited for your height and build.

Without a club, assume your golf stance and place your hands in a praying position, palms facing together. Now, lift your arms up, then let them drop, palms still together.

How Close Or How Far Should You Stand From The Ball?
Stages in establishing your natural stance.

Stage I

Stage II

Stage III

Repeat the exercise several times. You will note that your hands always fall the same distance away from your body. Depending on your build, the distance that separates the club from your body could range anywhere from six inches to ten inches. The important idea is to establish a position with which you feel most comfortable and at ease, without undue stretching or cramping of the arms. When you are establishing your natural club position, remember always to assume a "sitting" position on address. Lift the club up with your arms extended, keeping your hand pressure steady. Bring the club down slowly until it touches the ground. Repeat the movement several times. The club will hit the same place each time, indicating that you have found the position best suited for you.

Try repeating the above exercise assuming an upright, non-sitting position on address. Because of the stiffness of the upper body and arms, the club head will seldom return to the same place when it is lowered. It is crucial, therefore, that you always assume a "sitting" position to ensure minimum variation of club head position. Arm and hand muscles should be neither too tense nor too relaxed. The body should be alert and in control of the club at all times.

Positioning Your Head

"Keep your eye on the ball!" is one of the most revered traditional golfing commandments. Unfortunately, it is also one of the worst pieces of advice any golfer could follow! The last thing you want to do in golf is to concentrate on the ball! There are far too many other things to command your attention than the golf ball. After all, the ball can go nowhere without the express bidding of your body and your club. Your concentration should, therefore, be on coordinating the various movements of your body which, in turn, will move your club through the ball.

Just before you prepare to make a backswing, focus your left eye on or slightly behind the club head. Position your chin so that it is pointing toward your right knee. This movement will "set" your head in position and will keep it steady during the swing.

Since the head is the center of the swing axis, it must be kept perfectly still throughout the swing. The "setting" of the head just before you commence your swing will minimize any tendency you may have to move your head. A look at all of the successful women pros on tour today should demonstrate our point! Heads in the gallery may turn as they play, but theirs remain perfectly still!

Before beginning the backswing, focus your left eye on, or slightly behind, the club head. This will ensure a "set" head position throughout the swing.

CHAPTER THREE

YOUR GOLF SWING

The Backswing

Before beginning your backswing, run a checklist on your body position. Check your grip, stance and head position to see that they are aligned with the club. Next, set your hand pressure by lifting the club slightly off the ground, no more than 1/16 inch to 1/4 inch. Do not set the club down again, since the slight lifting movement will automatically set your correct hand pressure. The club head should barely touch the turf at the commencement of the backswing. Those of you who have followed the pros on tour, may have noticed that many of them lift the club head prior to the swing. Often, this movement is done so quickly that it is barely perceptible.

Having run through your pre-swing checklist, you are now ready to begin the backswing.

With your left shoulder, arm and hand leading, gently push the club head back and under in one unbroken movement. As you push under with your left hand, you will feel a slight bowing of your left wrist. The knuckles of your left hand should now be facing the ground.

Your left arm must be kept perfectly straight throughout the entire backswing. This is difficult and, at first, may feel awkward, but it is a skill that must be mastered. By keeping the left arm straight, you can maintain maximum control over the club during all phases of the backswing. Any relaxing or bending of the left arm will immediately cause lack of power and control and give the right hand an opportunity to dominate. Right hand dominance during the backswing is the major cause of poor, uncontrolled golf.

Although you may feel strained and unnatural trying to keep your left arm straight, your efforts will be rewarded by greatly improved golf. (If it is any consolation to you, keep in mind that to play golf well you must develop muscle controls that seem unnatural and uncomfortable. Be on guard when you begin to feel comfortable and at ease with your game. You are bound to be doing something wrong! In golf, the *hard* way is the *right* way. Alas, there is no Primrose Path to Par for any of us!)

At the beginning of the backswing, your club head should be squarely in line with the ball. Your left hand should push the club back and slightly under to maintain an unbroken line with the target. To turn the club "under," simply turn your left hand away from your body so that all of the knuckles are facing the ground.

The movement will, at first, feel strange and unnatural. You will experience a tremendous pull on your left arm as you progress back and then move through to the top of the backswing. The pulling effect on your left arm will cause your left wrist to bend or "cock" automatically at the top of your swing, readying the club head for its downward descent.

If you do not feel a pull on your left wrist at the top of the swing, most likely you have either (a) eased up on your hand pressure, (b) forgotten to push the club face under, or (c) let the right hand take over, jerking the club head off the line of flight. The following illustrations show the variation in the club head's line of flight during the back swing.

Keep reaching low and back with your swing as though someone were pulling your club head toward them. Once you have reached as far back as you can with your arms, then your shoulder and back automatically will turn your body up and away from your target. At this point, your club head should have made a perfect arc backward.

At the top of your backswing, your back should be turned toward the target. The upper part of your body also ought to be extended as far as your muscles will permit it to go. Upper body extension will vary according to the individual. To set the maximum limits to your backswing, determine the degree of extension that is best suited to your height and build.

PHASES OF THE BACK SWING

Phase I   A relaxed but firm set-up position.

Phase II   A low and slow take-off with left arm, hand and club forming an unbroken line.

Phase III   Left hand pushes club back and slightly under to maintain line with target.

Phase IV   Left wrist automatically cocks at top of swing.

The gradual torque or stretching of muscles during the backswing in golf is like the movement an archer makes as she tautens the bow in readiness to release the arrow. Like the archer, you must stretch your hands, arm, shoulder and back to prepare your club for its downward release. Do not let up or relax on the stretching movement. To do so in golf would be as fatal as the archer failing to stretch the bow sufficiently to release the arrow.

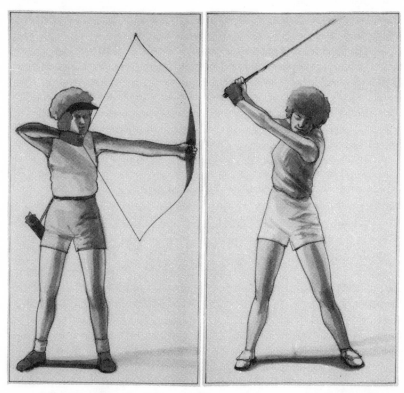

Like the archer, the golfer should experience a stretching of muscles as she extends into the backswing.

If you want to achieve maximum power in your backswing, you must establish a solid base. This is where the lower part of your body comes into play. The lower body must *resist* as you swing back. At the beginning of the swing, concentrate most of your weight on the center of your left foot. Your right foot should be bent inward, with a slight amount of weight on the right instep. Approximately 80 percent of your weight on address should be on your left side.

As you commence to swing, your left knee will pull in naturally toward your right knee. Your weight will then automatically transfer from the left foot to the inside of your right foot. At the top of the swing, your leg and hip muscles should be fully extended. All of your weight should bear down on your right hip and on the inside of your right foot.

It is important to remember that your right side should be kept firm but passive during the backswing. Hips and knee should not be thrown outward, since this will cause lack of control and subsequent loss of power. There should be little or no movement of the lower body during the backswing, except the natural movement caused by the stretching of your upper body muscles.

How far should you lift your left heel off the ground during the backswing?

The correct answer to this question will depend on your build, height, and general physical condition. Remember that the turn of your back and shoulder will automatically pull your heel off the ground. The movement will occur naturally and without your help!

If you are a muscular person, and give your shoulders a full turn, your left heel will automatically be lifted high off the ground. On the other hand, if you have a smaller physique, it is quite likely that your left heel will rise very little off the ground. Again, find out what is best for you. Do not try to copy anyone else's foot movements. Golf is a uniquely personal game of both mind-over-body and physical control. Only you can achieve that control, working within your own limits.

What happens to the right hand and arm during the backswing?

As we have explained in previous chapters, the function of the right hand and arm is to act as a support or brace for the left arm as it swings away from the ball. Your right hand should not lift or pull the club during the backswing. If the right hand does dominate the left and lift the club off the proper line, it will cause the club to slice through the ball. As noted in the chapter, YOUR GOLF CLINIC "Common Causes and Cures for Golf Ailments," the most common cause of slicing is an overly dominant right hand.

At the top of your backswing, your right elbow should point downward, not outward. Your right hand should support the left without exerting any undue pressure.

Building Distance, Power, And Accuracy Into Your Swing

Women golfers often complain that they cannot achieve distance in their golf game because they lack the necessary muscle power and build needed to give them distance. Such is not the case. Failure to achieve distance is not caused by lack of muscle or build — some of the finest women pros on tour are slightly built — but by lack of control in the swing. A sloppy, uncoordinated swing back and through the ball will lead to uncontrolled, inconsistent, and weak golf.

"Putting it all together" with the slow motion backswing.

As you seek to develop a fluid, well-executed swing you must learn to analyze and to control each phase of your swing. The correct stretching of muscles, distribution of weight, positioning of arms, hands and lower body, need to be carefully analyzed during each part of your swing. One of the best ways you can learn to coordinate your body movements is to practice each move in slow motion. Only by making deliberate, slow-motion moves will you be able to analyze each part of your swing and to feel the correct muscle movements.

At first, your slow motion backswing probably will feel strained and unnatural. This frequently creates a tendency to speed the process up. No matter how strong your inclination is, *do not* speed up that backswing! To do so will cause your hands to move too quickly, leaving your back and shoulders out of synchronization. Discipline yourself to gear your hands down to the speed of your back and shoulders, as they move away from the ball.

Slow and deliberate moves in the backswing will not only help you "put it all together" but it will train your muscles to "*keep* it all together" during the actual course of play.

By the way, next time you get the chance to follow the touring women pros, take a close look at their backswings. We know of very few who use -- and get away with! -- a fast backswing. "Slow it down and keep it slow" is the best advice we can give when it comes to your backswing. Learn to practice the slow motion swing by making only a half-swing. As you can see from the illustration below, the club head in a half-swing is level with your hips. Progress to a full swing only after you have mastered the half-swing.

What is meant by a "full" backswing?

A "full" backswing is the farthest distance your arms, shoulders, and back will carry you as you swing back. According to individual variations in height and physique, "full" swings can vary considerably. Some women golfers have relatively short and low backswings. Others have high and wide backswings. Both types of swings are equally effective if they are properly executed. Contrary to popular opinion, the length or fullness of the backswing has little or nothing to do with the distance you will hit the ball.

Many times, women golfers will try to get greater distance by over-swinging their club at the top of the backswing. Over-swinging is one of the most common faults of the woman golfer. Poor hand pressure or lack of right side control will cause the club to drop down at the top of the swing. As a result, the player loses power and control as she prepares to make her downswing from a weak position.

PHASES IN THE HALF BACKSWING

Right side should remain firm throughout the backswing. Note slight flexing of the right knee forward to provide maximum flexibility of upper body movement.

Phase I

Phase II

Phase III

Phase IV

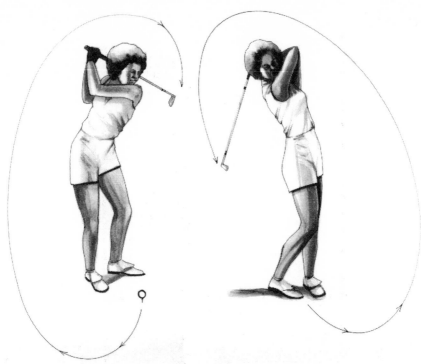

A weak, flat backswing with poor arm, hand and wrist control at the top of the swing leads to inconsistent, weak golf.

If you have a tendency to over-swing, try to cut down on the length of your backswing. It is better by far to underswing than over-swing.

The Forward Swing

Just as your backswing caused your body to move *away from* the target, so your forward swing will carry your body *toward* the target. At the top of the backswing, your body is poised, and ready to release the club head downward and through the ball. Always precede your forward or downward swing by making a slight bumping movement with your hip towards the target. You can make the move with either the right or the left hip. Be sure, however, that the hip moves no more than one inch maximum; otherwise, you will lose balance. The slight movement of your hip will start an immediate transfer of weight from your right side to the left. It is this transfer of weight which gives your club head the needed momentum to move through the ball.

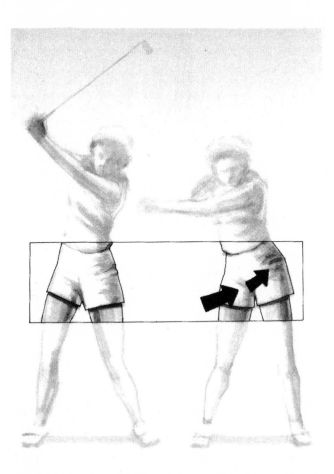

A slight, almost imperceptible "bump" of the hips toward the target area should begin your forward or down swing. Remember that the lower body should start the downward movement and not your arms and hands!

Never begin your forward swing with your arms and hands! To do so will leave your weight centered on your right side as your arms move through the ball. Loss of power, balance and control will result.

Once you have made the slight hip movement, immediately twist your stomach round toward the target. The combination of hip and stomach twist will automatically cause your arms to move downward. Your right knee will release from its locked position and move in toward your left foot. The combined movements of your hip, stomach and knee will, as a result, give your club head momentum, thus enabling it to move powerfully through the ball. Hand pressure should be kept constant throughout the downswing. Undue tension or a weakening of pressure can cause power loss and a lack of accuracy.

The Follow Through

The follow through or finish to your golf swing is an important indicator which tells you what has taken place during the actual swing. If your lower body has led the way through the ball and if your hand pressure has kept constant throughout, you will attain a good, well-balanced finish naturally. At the end of your swing, your body will be pointing towards the target, as shown below.

PHASES OF THE FORWARD SWING:

Indoor Drill

Phase I

Phase II

Phase III

Phase IV

It's an excellent idea to work on your game by going through slow-motion movements indoors. The above sequential photographs stress the need for lower body lead in the down swing. Note the good extension of arms, hands and club as they move through the ball.

A poorly executed swing, caused either by lack of lower body movement or by poor hand pressure will lead to a weak follow through.

Finding Your Swing Tempo

No matter how fine a swing you develop in golf, it cannot reach its fullest potential without a set tempo or rhythm which will carry your body back and then through the ball. There are two factors which will determine the tempo of your swing:

1. Your general physical condition and muscle tone, and
2. The rate of speed with which you can smoothly and comfortably move back and through the ball without losing balance or control.

Your Backswing Tempo

To determine the speed of the backswing best suited for you, stand in front of a mirror, club in hand. Assume a full address position. With a deliberate slow motion swing, reach low and back. Turn your upper body to complete a full backswing. Check your position in the mirror. Is your left arm straight? Is your left wrist cocked? Are your hip and right knee firm? Is your right elbow pointing downward? Once you have satisfied yourself that all phases of your backswing are correct, then repeat all of the movements using a slightly faster swing. You will soon establish the tempo which will give you maximum control over your swing without losing your balance. Many women find it helpful during practice sessions to repeat the words, "Reach and Turn," as they perform the backswing. The repetition of the words will help you attain and retain a slow, well-modulated backswing.

As we previously have stated, many golfers tend to take an overly fast backswing. No matter how confident you are with your game, it is always a good idea to run an occasional check on the tempo of your backswing. The Ancient Romans had a phrase for it: FESTINA LENTE. "Make haste slowly."

Your Forward Swing Tempo

The tempo of your forward swing will be determined by the speed with which you can release your hips, stomach, and knee through the ball. The "hip and twist" action you make through the ball on the downswing should take relatively less time to perform than does the "reach and turn" movement of your backswing. The downward "release" movement of the club from the top of the backswing will obviously be faster than the deliberate slow-motion tautening of the muscles in the backswing. Once you have determined the speed at which you can perform the hip and twist movement without losing control or balance, then you will have established the downswing tempo best suited for you.

Your Swing Arc

Are you a "swinger" or a "hitter" on the golf course? Unless you have the muscle and slugging power of an Arnold Palmer, we recommend that you learn to *swing* at the ball, rather than *hit* at it! Many golfers mistakenly believe that golf is a game of brute force. Their aim is to "kill" the ball -- frequently with disastrous results! Distance is not the name of the golf game. A well-coordinated, carefully executed swing is the key to success in golf.

In previous chapters, we have covered the various parts of the golf swing. Putting these parts together should find you and your club center-stage of a one and one-half arc performance!

The following suggestion should help you achieve a perfect back arc swing. When you address the ball, consciously reach slightly forward with your left hand. As you begin your back swing, try to keep your left hand as far away from your left arm as possible. This will help you attain a "reaching" effect with your club during the backswing. Do not let up on the "reach" as you swing back and then through the ball. Any letting up or relaxing of the "reach" will break the arc of your swing and bring the right hand into play.

Should your club head trace the same arc forward as it did backward?

We hope not! Otherwise, you would completely lose your balance and topple forward because all of your weight would be on your toes!

You will recall that at the top of the swing, you began your down swing with a coordinated hip-stomach-knee movement. The turn and twist move automatically turned your body round and toward the target. As you redirect your body at the top of the backswing, the line of your club will automatically be redirected. Your club will be pulled slightly in and back from the upper arc line.

As your club head swings down, it will therefore make an *inside-out* full arc as it moves through and out from the ball.

Always try to maneuver the club head out and away from the ball at impact. This movement will negate any tendency you may have to bring the club back in toward your body at the end of the swing. By consciously pushing out and away from the ball, your arms and club will complete the forward arc in a full, high position.

A poorly extended, flat back swing and subsequent weak follow through will lead to chronic slicing.

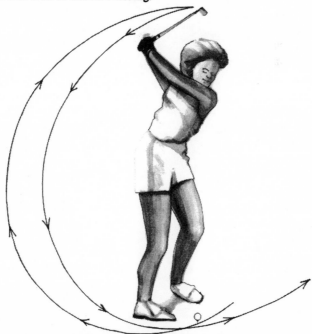

A wide, extended arc on the back swing with proper transferral of weight at the top of the swing creates an inside-out full arc as the club moves through the ball.

CHAPTER FOUR

YOUR LONG AND SHORT GAME

The Long Irons

The Numbers 2, 3, and 4 irons are known as the "long irons." They are designed to give you maximum distance when you hit the ball off the fairway towards the green. Because they have relatively long shafts and small heads, the long irons are regarded by many women golfers as difficult clubs to use. There is no reason why this should be so. If a woman can effectively swing and control a Number 7 iron, it should logically follow that she should be able to use a Number 3 iron with equal skill and effectiveness.

Remember that the dynamics of your golf swing should not vary, no matter which club you use. The basic principles you apply to good, short iron play also apply to long irons. It is true, however, that long irons do call for a greater degree of control because of their additional shaft length.

Here are several approaches and techniques which, if properly used, should help to improve your long iron play.

1. Play the ball from approximately one inch inside of your left heel. Turn your left toe 45 degrees toward the target. This positioning of your feet will enable you to make a longer back arc and will give you greater momentum as you move through the ball. Your right foot should point directly forward and should be positioned directly underneath the inside of your right shoulder.

2. When you prepare to hit a long iron shot, always position your club head in line with the target. Then, line up your feet so that the heels are parallel with your club head. You will now have made two tracks. Your club track will point directly towards the hole, while your body track will point slightly to the left of the hole. If you are lined up correctly, your body will be pointing to the left of the target, while your club head will aim directly at the target. A good rule of thumb for iron play is to *aim left* in order to *hit right* of the target. By doing so, you will avoid the tendency many golfers have to play to the right of the target because they think that their body is pointing too far to the left!

3. Prepare yourself mentally to make a full arc during your backswing with a long iron. The length of the shaft will require you to do so. Do not let up on left arm and hand control of the club as you reach back. The long shaft will automatically create more arc and leverage in your swing. This increased leverage will call for greater control on your part. Don't let the position of the club head collapse or sag at the top of your swing.

Strange as it may sound, there is no reason why, during practice sessions, you cannot take your eye off the ball as you check the various moves in your back swing. Study each phase of the swing back, then look at your position at the top of the swing. After you are satisfied that everything is in order, then focus your eye slightly behind the ball and commence your downswing.

As we have stated before, the ball is going nowhere without your express bidding! The relation of player to ball in golf differs greatly from other sports such as baseball or tennis. The golf ball will always be moving away from you, rather than toward you. Never be in a rush to hit the ball. No one is going to drive or throw it at you expecting you to hit it!

4. Try to avoid the temptation to lift your body up as the club moves down and through the ball. Keep your body low and avoid any jerking or scooping with your hands. It is the club head which will lift the ball and not your hands or wrists.

Keep in mind that in long iron play you must hit *down* on the ball before you can lift it *up*. Failure to hit down will result in topping the ball.

5. The tremendous satisfaction you will get from hitting consistently and well with the long irons can only come after concentrated periods of practice. Always practice your long irons using a half swing. Swing back to your hip level, twist, and move your lower body through the ball. "Back, stretch, hip and twist" are the essential elements of a smooth, rhythmic golf swing. Never try to "kill" the ball. Power and distance will be achieved naturally once you have learned to move your hips, stomach, and knee down into and through the ball.

6. Psychologically, many golfers are at a definite disadvantage with long iron play. They *know* that the club is designed to hit the ball long distances. Subconsciously, they tense their hands and arms as they prepare for "the kill." The result, all too often, is a punched or squeezed long iron shot which fails to go long distances.

If you are having problems with long irons, try the following suggestion. Shorten your grip on the club so that your hands are positioned just above the bottom of the grip. Now swing the club as though it were a Number 7 iron. Take a smooth, controlled half swing back and through the ball. DO NOT TRY TO GET DISTANCE. Concentrate on moving your body through the ball with emphasis on a good lower body movement. Continue to use a short grip until you have achieved *complete control* over the club. Gradually, increase the length of your grip, without letting up on control of the club. Forget distance as you learn to become master (or mistress!) of the long iron. A well executed swing, with excellent lower body movement, will soon have the club doing all of the work for you.

The Woods

The "Driver" Or Number One Wood

Those of us who watch the pros on TV are constantly reminded of the old golf maxim: "You drive for show and putt for dough." There is no denying the excitement we all experience watching a 6'2", 250-pounder whack the ball 280 yards down the fairway! However, unless you are 6'2", weigh 250 pounds, and play golf seven days a week for a living, we recommend that you forget those 280-yard drives! Be realistic about your game off the tee. Know your own strengths and play to them. Just keep in mind that it's a far, far better thing to hit the ball 150 yards down the center of the fairway, than to belt it 200 yards, wildly veering to the left or right and heading smack into trouble!

The following suggestions should help you develop effective techniques for consistently good tee shots.

1. Tee the ball so that at least one-half of it appears about the club face. Check the turf immediately behind the ball for bumps or indentations which could interfere with the smooth path of your backswing.

2. Put your feet together before preparing to address the ball. Move your right foot so that it is lined with the inside of your right shoulder. The ball should be positioned either out from the center of the left toe or off the left instep. Either position is correct. Choose the one which is best for you. Remember to turn the left toe slightly to the left of the target. This movement will give you a slightly "open" stance which will allow your lower body to move through the ball with greater ease. Your right foot should remain straight, giving you a solid base as you move into the backswing.

3. Assume a "sitting" position, then stretch your left arm slightly forward, as if you were "reaching" for the ball. Lift the club face slightly off the ground to establish your correct hand pressure before beginning your backswing.

4. The driver has the longest shaft of all your clubs. As you stretch back and into your full backswing, you should feel a tremendous pull as your body carries the club in a full arc to the top of the swing. Your wrists should be fully "cocked." Your lower body should be ready to drive your hip, stomach, and knee into and through the ball.

5. Because the driver is a relatively long and heavy club, you probably will feel the natural tendency to "muscle" the club with your hands and arms in the down swing. It is your hips, stomach and knee which should lead the club through the ball -- not your hands and arms. As we have pointed out previously, too much arm and hand domination in the downswing can cause numerous problems in your game.

If you have a psychological hang-up with the driver, try "choking" or shortening your grip on the shaft. As we recommended for the long

USING YOUR DRIVER EFFECTIVELY

Important positions in the back swing.

Phase I

Phase II

Phase III

Phase IV

Phase V

Phase VI

Important positions in the follow through and finish.

Phase I

Phase II

Phase III

Phase IV

Phase V

irons, learn to swing the driver as though it were a Number 7 iron. Concentrate on attaining a smooth, well-coordinated swing. Purposely try to hit the ball "soft" -- that is, do not try to get distance. Repeat your short swing over and over again until you have complete control. Then slightly increase the length of your grip until you have a full grip -- and full control over your club!

The Fairway Woods

Diamonds may be a girl's best friend, but your fairway woods should come in a close second! As we mentioned in previous chapters, the Number 5 wood is a favorite with many women pros. If you have been having difficulties with your fairway woods, try using the Number 5 wood for a while. The relatively short shaft of the Number 5 makes it easy to control as you swing back and through the ball. The slant of the club face will help you lift the ball clean and high off the turf.

Many of the same rules that apply to your long irons also apply to your fairway woods. Here is a quick review.

1. Play the ball approximately one inch off the inside of your left foot. Point your left foot slightly to the left of the target in order to avoid ankle strain as you turn through the ball.

2. Stretch your left arm slightly forward towards the ball at address. The "reaching" movement of your left arm should not cause the

arm to become tense and stiff. It should, however, give your club additional extension or "reach" in the backswing.

3. Your left eye should be focused slightly behind the club head, and your chin should point towards your right knee. Remember to keep your head upright, so that it will not impede your left shoulder as it pivots around during the backswing.

4. Psychologically prepare yourself to make a full arc with the club. The length of the shaft will give you full back extension. Never let up on your left arm and hand pressure during the backswing. Remember that your right hand will be only too glad to take over if your left hand lets it do so!

5. Since you do not have the benefit of a tee when you use woods on the fairway, it is very important that you move your club head down and through the ball in order to loft it. Your fairway woods and long irons both call for excellent lower body movement. As with your long irons, try to avoid the "lifting up" of your body, arms and hands as you swing into the ball.

If you are having problems lofting the ball with your fairway woods, you might try out the following idea during practice sessions. Tee up the ball and hit it with your Number 3 wood. Continue to use a tee until you feel confident with the wood. As you continue practice, gradually push the tee further into the ground. Eventually, the tee should be completely in the ground but, psychologically, you will still be hitting at the ball using a tee!

Your Short Game

It has often been said -- and rightly so -- that more golf games are won on and around the putting surface than on any other part of the course. The thrilling finishes we often see in pro games seldom start with the drive from the tee. A beautifully executed chip and carefully timed putt more often than not will enchant the gallery and win the purse!

Touch and not muscle are the important elements in your short game. Women golfers are often at an advantage in the short game because of their "feel" for the shorter clubs. Psychologically, you also are at an advantage with short irons because their relatively short shafts help you maintain better control.

The Pitching Wedge

The pitching wedge, or Number 10 iron, and the sand wedge have the heaviest head weights of all the irons. The extra weight and loft of the club face makes the pitching wedge an excellent club to use when the ball is embedded in heavy grass. Because of its heavy head weight, the wedge enables you to hit down on the ball more, giving the shot greater "bite." The shaft of the pitching wedge is short. You will want to take a narrow stance, therefore, when you use the wedge. Play the ball either from the inside of your left foot or slightly from left of center.

There are several techniques you will want to keep in mind as you use the pitching wedge.

1. Because of the heaviness of the head, you will get twice as much wrist cock with the wedge as you would with other irons. Avoid weak or loose wrist movements. Keep your wrists firm as your lower body moves through the ball.

2. The length of the backswing you make with a wedge will depend on the distance you are from the putting surface. A quarter swing will carry your club to knee level; a half swing to hip level; and a three quarter swing to shoulder level.

The amount of wrist movement you get will depend on the length of your backswing. There will be very little wrist cock in a quarter backswing. On the other hand, a three quarter and full swing will require considerable cocking of the wrists. Firm arm and wrist control are essential to a well-executed wedge shot.

3. It is important that you maintain constant hand pressure throughout the wedge shot. Many golfers, in an attempt to loft the ball, subconsciously tense their arms and hands as they move into the ball. Any tensing will immediately result in your body and club lifting up, thus bringing about a topped golf shot.

A close look at touring women pros will often show them taking turf or making a divot with a wedge shot. Taking turf is the sign of a well-executed wedge shot. Constant hand pressure and good lower body movement will take the club head down and into the ball. After the ball has been hit, the club head still continues its descent into the ground, taking a divot with it on the upswing.

4. It is vital that you keep your head as still as possible when you make pitching wedge shots. Because the wedge has such a relatively short shaft, your swing arc will be quite short. As a result, your body will not swivel around quite as much. Any upward pulling of your head will jerk the body and club head up and away from the ball. Hold your head up and as still as possible to achieve maximum effect with your wedge shots.

The Sand Wedge

The happiness that a three year old experiences playing *in* the sand, can only be equalled by the happiness (and relief!) we experience upon playing successfully *out* of the sand! The sand trap, alas, is a source of difficulty for many women golfers. It need not be, however, if a few basic facts are kept constantly in mind.

1. The sand wedge differs from the pitching wedge because of a flange running along the sole of the club. If you were to position the head

of the sand wedge on the ground, you would see that the flange juts out from the sole of the club.

It is the flange which helps you blast the sand and move the ball out of the trap. To execute a successful wedge shot, it is essential that the club head hit the *sand* first. Never hit the *ball* first, that is, *unless* the sand is so wet that the ball is resting cleanly on top of it and you don't need to take sand with it. It is the force of the sand which gives the ball momentum to travel high and out of the trap.

2. If you have a fairly short shot of, say eight to ten feet, you should aim your club head to hit the sand one inch to two inches behind the ball. Aiming the club so that it will hit behind the ball enables you to make a full swing. The ball will then be lifted high and will stop faster because of the braking effect of the sand. Since golf rules do not permit you to place or ground the club head in the sand at address, it is a good idea to establish your hand pressure prior to entering the trap. Simply lift the club 1/4 inch off the surface until you establish pressure on the first three fingertips of your left hand. Take a few practice swings to loosen up prior to making the sand shot.

3. When you address the ball, shuffle your feet around in the sand. The "digging" movement of your feet will settle your weight on your heels and give you the needed balance as you swing back, down, and through the ball. A slight "sitting" movement before you begin the swing will give you additional stability.

4. Always take an open stance for sand shots, placing most of your weight on your left side.

5. Do not tighten up on your hand pressure during the sand shot. Remember that it is the *club* and not your hands which will scoop the sand and the ball out of the bunker.

6. More often than not, you will use very little lower body movement in a sand shot. This is because in most instances you will not be taking a full swing unless your ball either is buried in the sand or unless you are 30 yards or so away from the green. Swing low and back, keeping your head perfectly still. Always swing down and through the sand, and avoid the urge you may feel to jerk your body and club head up.

7. Psychologically, it is better to think "flange" than "ball" when you play out of a trap. As you approach to make the shot, visualize the picture of the flange cutting through the sand and blasting the ball. On address, focus your left eye on the area back of the ball where your club head will strike the sand. Then swing your club back and through the sand with a fluid, smooth motion. Do not rush your swing.

8. If your ball is lying in wet, heavy sand, try using a pitching wedge rather than a sand wedge to chip it out. The flange of the sand wedge will dig too much into the wet sand, thus creating a loss of power as the club moves through the ball.

Sometimes, when your ball is lying close to the edge of a trap which has little or no lip, you may want to use a putter to get the ball out of the trap. Remember, however, that you cannot ground any club during sand trap play.

SOME HINTS ON SAND SHOTS

- Relax! Sand play is no more difficult than wedge play. Getting up-tight leads to a poorly executed golf shot.

- Be prepared to move smoothly back and through the ball. Don't increase your swing tempo.

- Take an open stance. This will enable your body to move through the ball with ease.

- Take a short grip on your sand wedge especially if the trap is close to the putting surface.

- Keep your knees flexed. This will enable you to stay low as you move through the ball.

- Keep your eye on the sand immediately behind the ball. Stay down as you move through the sand. Try to avoid looking up since this will lead to a jerking movement of the body.

- A half swing is usually adequate for a sand shot. Be sure that your wrists and knees are relaxed for maximum flexibility.

Sand Play

Phase I

Phase II

Phase III

Phase IV

Phase V

Putting

It has sometimes been suggested that there are really two golf games: Golf and Putting.

Just as a canoe will make little progress if you lack skill with a paddle, so your golf game will get nowhere without good putting techniques. Before we discuss these techniques, let's look at some interesting statistics.

On a regulation par-3 hole, two out of three strokes, or 66 percent of your score, is made by the putter.

On a regulation par-4 hole, two out of four strokes, or 50 percent of your score, is made by the putter.

On a regulation par-5 hole, two out of five strokes, or 40 percent of your score, is made by the putter.

Put another way, if you were to par 18 holes on a regulation course, approximately one half on your score would be made with your putter. Of the fourteen clubs in your golf bag, the putter is by far your most important, and most used club.

Just how successful you are on the putting green will depend on how long you are willing to practice your putting game. There is no one, infallible approach, to successful putting. Indeed, there are almost as many putting theories and methods as there are pros on the tour! In some ways, you name your own game in putting -- but this should not be done until you are aware of some of the fundamental techniques which are essential to success on the putting green.

1. It's always a good idea to start studying your putting stroke before you get to the putting surface. Look at the slant of the green. Does it slope to the left or to the right? If you are playing with the ocean to your right, remember that the winds most often blow inland, thus causing the grass to grow right to left. If you are playing with mountains on your left, the terrain and grass are most likely to have a left to right slope. The slope of the green and grass will influence the distance and direction of your putting stroke.

2. Once you are on the putting surface, step behind your ball. Crouch down so that you have a "worms-eye view" of the line your ball will take as it heads toward the hole. Allow for any obvious slopes or biases to the left or right. If no slopes are perceptible, head the ball straight for the hole.

3. Play the ball either in line with your left toe or from the inside of your left instep. Your feet should be only slightly apart, and most of your weight should be on the left side and heels. Focus your left eye directly over the ball.

4. Many kinds of grips are used in putting. There are, however, some fundamentals you should keep in mind about the putting grip. To maintain better control during the putting stroke, keep your right thumb straight down the center of the shaft in a 12 o'clock position. The back of your left hand should always face the hole during the execution of the entire stroke. Both elbows should be held fairly close to your body.

5. Always keep the face of the putter square to the target! Take the club head back low and slowly, your left hand and putter head both pointing toward the target. You should have a minimum amount of wrist movement in putting (except in very short putts). It is your arms which should guide the club head back and through the ball.

6. Never "hit" a ball on the putting surface. Always "stroke" it. A slow, smooth stroking action of club to ball is the keynote to good putting.

Your Short Putting Game

To achieve maximum control over your short putts, try shortening your grip and narrowing your stance. When you hit a short putt, imagine that you are putting between two walls: The right "wall" extends in a line from your right foot, while the left "wall" extends from your left foot. The right "wall" will stop your putter as it moves back, thus keeping the club in line with your right foot. The left "wall" will stop your club head immediately after it hits the ball. This will bring about a slight bumping or jabbing motion as your putter pushes the ball toward the hole. In short putts of three feet or less, use your wrists to take the putter back and through the ball.

No matter how strong the temptation, never look up on your short putts! To do so will cause your body to jerk upward and you will top the ball.

Stay low on the ball at all times to achieve a smooth stroke. If it helps any, think of the putter head as a "worm scanner," moving back and forward slowly in search of friendly worms! We can't guarantee that you will find the worms, but we think you will vastly improve your putting stroke by keeping that putter head low!

Your Long Putting Game

A longer grip and wider stance are best for longer putts. Unlike the short putt, you should have a fairly long back stroke and follow through on the long putt. Strive to develop a low, smooth stroke back and through the ball when you make long putts. It's an excellent idea to experiment with various lengths of your putting stroke to determine the distance your ball will travel in relation to the length of the stroke. Again, we urge that you avoid trying to "hit" the ball in order to get distance. Any power you get on the putting green will come from your control of club over ball.

SOME HINTS ON PUTTING

- Start "reading" a putt as you approach the putting surface. Note the contours of the green and the condition of the grass. For example, if it's very dry, newly watered, freshly seeded, wet or soggy, etcetera.

- On very long putts don't spend a lot of time trying to read the green. Establish a general line and hit the ball. Concentrate on getting the ball as close to the hole as possible. Remember: Never up, never in!

- Tempo is all important in putting. Relax and keep an even, smooth tempo back and through the ball. "Low and slow" is the name of this game.

- Be conscious of hand pressure, especially if you have an assertive right hand which wants to take over and push the putt! Hand pressure should be kept even throughout the putt.

- As a general rule of thumb, think "arms" on long putts and "wrists" on short putts.

Putting

Phase I

Phase II

Phase III

Phase IV

-66-

Phase V

CHAPTER FIVE

YOUR GOLF CLINIC: CAUSES AND CURES FOR THE MOST COMMON GOLFING AILMENTS

We're sure you have heard the story of the two women golfers who were talking in the clubhouse one day about their respective games. "What's your handicap, Mabel?" asked one woman golfer. "My clubs, honey. All fourteen of them!" replied her exasperated companion.

Whether we are pro or amateur, week-end golfer or seven-days-a-week-twelve-months-a-year golfer, each one of us has experienced the frustration which comes from playing consistently poor golf. There are "those days" for all of us, when we *think* we are doing the right thing, but the ball just won't do what we want it to do. The ultimate frustration, alas, comes when we play consistently poor golf week after week, and month after month, repeating our mistakes with exasperating regularity. Under these conditions, golf ceases to be an enjoyable sport and becomes a source of drudgery. There is no reason why this should be so. If you are a chronic slicer, your slice can be cured. If hooking or topping or sclaffing are your problems, these too can be rather quickly remedied.

The following causes and cures for your golfing ailments cover the most common problems which beset the average golfer. While we hope to be able to help cure your particular problem, we also urge that you seek the advice of a professional golfer. Only by having a professional watch you swing, will you be able to identify specifically the cause and cure for a particular problem. The few dollars you spend with a professional will more than reward you with the satisfaction of an improved golf game.

Beware of the helpful -- and usually free! -- advice of well-meaning golfing friends. Unless they are professional golfers who can objectively analyze your swing, politely decline any help from the amateur circuit. As Grandmother used to say: "There's always free cheese in a mousetrap!"

Slicing

A sliced shot in golf is one which starts out straight then curves sharply off to the right. Slicing is by far the most common of all the golfing ailments. Small wonder, then, that when golf course architects design a course, they invariably put problem areas to the golfers' right. That is because they know that a legion of chronic slicers will be on the move heading for trouble on the right flank!

What causes a slice? There are many reasons why you slice a ball. The most common condition which leads to a slice, however, occurs when you change the arc of your downswing from inside-out to outside-in.

Slicing

Your club head cuts through the ball in an outside-in motion causing the ball to spin out and to the right.

Slicing most often occurs with the long woods and irons. The reason for this is simple: When you play a long club, you subconsciously prepare yourself to "kill" the ball. At the top of your backswing, the right hand takes over and jerks the club head outside the swing arc. You have no alternative but to swing down from a weak outside position. Your hands will move ahead of the lower body and cut the club head across the ball causing you and the ball to "go bananas" -- that is, to follow a banana-shaped curve to the right.

What can you do to cure a slice? Get back to the basics! First, check the line of your backswing. To do so, lay a club on the gound, pointing it toward the target. Swing back, following the line of the club. At the top of your swing run a checklist on your position. Is your left arm straight? Are your wrists cocked? Is your right elbow pointing downward? Is your weight centered on your right side? Do you have full upper left torso extension? Are your shoulders and back pointing toward the target?

Once you are satisfied with all phases of your backswing, concentrate on your lower body movements. Remember how vital it is that your lower body lead the way through the ball. Don't let your hands and arms take over. They will follow naturally after you make a good hip and twist movement which brings the club head down and through the ball in an inside-outside arc.

Some golfers try to cure their slice by experimenting with various grips and stances. Since the main source of the slice is a faulty swing-arc, it follows that switching grips and altering stances will do nothing to cure the slice! Often, all you will be doing is aggravating an already bad problem. Again, we urge that you get back to the basics. Check your left hand position on the club. Are your left arm, hand and club forming one, unbroken unit? Is the pressure on the fingertips of the first three fingers of your left hand?

Never take your right hand for granted. Always keep in mind that your right hand will take over if you let up on your left hand pressure. In a well-executed golf swing, the right hand and arm are supportive but passive partners with the left.

Hooking

A hooked golf shot is one which causes the ball to start out straight then curve sharply to the left. The hook is, therefore, the opposite of the slice and can be just as fatal if it is not controlled.

Occasionally, golfers confuse a hook with a draw. A drawn shot in golf is one in which the ball starts to the right then curls slightly to the left. If you have ever watched professional golf on TV, and have followed the ball's trajectory after a well hit drive, your eyes do not deceive you when you see the ball curve slightly to the left at the end of its flight. A drawn shot in golf is the neon sign which identifies the excellent golfer who knows how to control her club through the ball, hitting right and drawing left.

What causes a hooked golf shot? First, we should say that if you are a hooker, be a happy one! The hook is the sign of a golfer who has a great deal of potential which, if properly channeled, can be used to the golfer's advantage. If you hook the ball, in all probability you have an overly dominant left hand and wrist. While we urge left hand and arm control, the hooker has too much left hand and wrist movement as she swings through the ball. The over-dominance of the left hand and wrist at the point of impact causes the club face to close and a hooked shot results.

How do you cure a hook? Concentrate on solid arm, hand, and wrist movement as your lower body turns and brings your arms through the ball in the down swing. Always try to think of the club as an extension of your left arm, hand and wrist. You will break that line if your left wrist and hand snap the club face closed as you move into the ball. Try to keep the left arm, wrist and hand as one unit with the club as you guide the club through the ball. You will then achieve a rolling effect with your left arm as you follow through on your swing. Sometimes, a hook will occur when the golfer lets up on her left hand pressure at point of impact, letting the right hand take over at the last minute. The club face will then be snapped shut and a hooked shot will result. Sustained left hand pressure is vital to a well-executed golf shot.

Topping

Next to slicing, topping the ball is one of the most common problems in golf, especially for the beginning golfer. Topping occurs when the club head is jerked up at point of impact causing the ball to be hit by the sole of the club rather than the face.

A topped golf shot.

What causes a topped golf shot? There are several areas within your golf swing which, if faulty, can cause a topped ball. Mainly, however, the topped golf shot occurs when the player tries to lift the ball by scooping the club up and through the ball with her hands. It is perhaps one of the most difficult things for the golfer to keep in mind that it is *the club* and *not* the arms and hands which will lift the ball up. Why should you do all the work when the club manufacturer has already done it for you?

How can you cure topping? The following tips on topping should help you identify the most common problem areas which lead to topped shots.

1. When you address the ball, remember always to assume a "sitting" position. Maintain that position throughout the shot. This will

enable you to stay down on the ball and negate any desire you may have to jerk your body up at point of impact.

2. Failure to make a proper transfer of weight from right to left in the down swing will almost always result in a topped shot. With your weight still on the right side, your hands will lead the way through the ball, leaving the weight still on the right side. Think *"left, down and through"* as you make your down swing.

3. Beware of your right hand! Your anxiety to pick the ball up with the club can all too frequently lead to the right hand trying to scoop the ball up. As we have said before: Let the club do the work.

Sclaffing

Sclaffing – a word of ancient Scottish origin -- occurs when you hack up more than your fair share of the golf course! A sclaffed ball is one that is hit from too far behind. The club head strikes the turf first then moves into the ball. Jarred wrists frequently result from a sclaffed shot as the club head digs into the turf.

Since the causes for sclaffing and topping are closely related, the cures for both are essentially the same. Here are some pointers which can help if sclaffing is your problem.

1. Be sure that you transfer your weight from right to left in the down swing. Move your lower body through the ball without trying to "muscle" it with your right hand.

A sclaffed golf ball.

2. Check the position of your arms at the beginning of the swing. You could be standing too close to the ball. Your arms should extend forward naturally away from your body and should not be cramped in close to your sides. Remember to "reach" slightly forward as you address the ball and maintain the reaching effect during the entire backswing.

3. Run a check on your stance. You may be playing the ball too far forward of center. This will result in the club head hitting the ground too soon at the bottom of the down arc. Take a few practice swings to determine where your club head makes contact with the turf, then adjust your stance accordingly.

Uneven Lies

Nothing can be more boring to the golfer than to play on a course which has endlessly flat terrain with nary a molehill in sight for relief! The pleasure we all experience in playing on a beautifully sculptured course with undulating terrain does much to add to the challenge and enjoyment of golf. Don't let these uphill and downhill lies pall your pleasure! Approach uneven lies with a prior knowledge of what you will do to compensate for the unevenness of your position, then play accordingly.

If you have an uphill lie, you will tend to hook or pull the ball to the left. To compensate, simply aim more to the right of the target area. You will have the tendency also to play short of the target area because of your uphill position, so take one club stronger or lower in number. Try to keep your weight on the left to compensate for the strong right pull. Play the ball off your left foot or inside of your left instep for maximum follow through.

If you have a downhill lie, your body will want to jerk up as you move through the ball. A topped ball will result. You will also have the tendency to push the ball to the right because of your downhill position. Purposely play to the left of your target area and try to keep *down* on the ball as much as possible. Play the ball either center or slightly to the right of center of your feet.

Psychologically, it may be to your advantage in downhill lies to play with a club which has a fairly open face. The shorter shaft and greater loft of the face will give you greater control as you move down and through the ball.

Shanking

A shanked shot occurs when the club face strikes the ball on the neck of the club instead of in the center of the club face. As a result, the ball veers sharply to the right or to the left, sometimes almost at a ninety degree angle.

Shanked shots occur most often when the arms and hands push the club face out and away at impact, thus breaking the line of the downward arc and resulting in the ball being hit by the club neck instead of the club face.

If you have a tendency to shank, concentrate on developing a smooth, rhythmical lower body movement through the ball. Try to keep your hand pressure constant as your club face moves through the ball. Don't let your eagerness to hit the ball cause your hands to jerk or push the club forward at impact. Just remember that it is impossible to shank the ball if your lower body and hands are moving in smooth coordination.

A shanked golf shot.

Concentration

What do you think about when you hit a golf ball? About what you heard about Sally Smith when you were in the clubhouse? About those dreadful Schlossgonheimenstrasser's who moved in next door with their Irish wolfhound puppy? About whose lawn the Irish wolfhound puppy is now on?

No matter how fascinating your thoughts may be at other times, we hope that while you are playing golf you will concentrate all of your mental energies on your game. Sad to relate but true, the minds of a majority of golfers go entirely blank when they hit a golf ball. Make a quick survey of your golfing friends and ask them what they think about when they swing a golf club. Don't be surprised when you hear the response: "Nothing." One thing is subconsciously present in the minds of most golfers as they prepare to hit the golf ball. *Distance.* With that thought uppermost in mind, the golfer then proceeds to hit – not swing at! – the ball. Any prior thought she may have given to control of her swing, quickly disappears as she sets out for "the kill." There's a bit of Jekyll and Hyde in all of us golfers. So next time you go out to play, why not leave mindless Hyde at home with that Irish wolfhound puppy and take the thoughtful Jekyll as your companion on the links!

Since golf is a game of mind over body control, your entire concentration during the swing must be on the movement, form, and tempo of your swing in its entirety. As you step up to the ball before each shot, go through a mental checklist. Set your correct grip, hand pressure and stance. Sit back and get ready to swing. Consciously follow each phase of your swing back and through the ball. At the end of each swing, you should be able to account for each movement you made during the swing: "Reach and turn, twist and through." If you cannot remember each of these movements in a golfer's mantra, then you probably didn't make them!

A look at the touring pros should convince you of the tremendous need we golfers have for concentration on each shot we make. No matter how good one is, mind over body control must be maintained at all times. Golf is not an easy game, and it never becomes one. If the pros make it all *look* easy, that is because they spend endless hours concentrating on all phases of their game.

How good are your powers of concentration? Next time you are out practicing, try closing your eyes as you make the entire swing. Concentrate all of your thoughts on the various moves your body will make as you swing back and through the ball. If you have good control and an accurate muscle memory and response, you will hit the ball as well, if not better, than if your eyes had been opened.

Next time you watch some of our best touring pros hit the ball with seeming ease, you may think to yourself: "I bet she could do that with her eyes closed!" And you'd probably be right!

How To Practice Your Golf Game

What practice is not

Contrary to the belief of many golfers, practice is not standing on a golf driving range and hitting one or two buckets of balls. That is confusing practice with exercise. Frequently, alas, it is also exercise of the worst kind, since it could promote bad golfing habits through constant repetition.

What practice is

Practice is a concentrated, coordinated effort to improve either one specific part of your golf swing or specific parts of your golf game.

Practice is, in effect, the perfection of movement you wish to attain during actual play in a golf game.

How to practice

Get a small -- not large! -- bucket of balls. Set the balls ten to twelve paces behind you so that you have to walk to the bucket after each practice shot. Why walk? Because the pause between each shot more closely parallels what takes place during your actual golf game: Hit, walk, assess your shot. The pause you take between shots will give you the opportunity to analyze each movement you made during the practice shot. Learn to question yourself constantly during practice sessions.

Many teaching pros recommend the use of a Number 7 iron during practice sessions. The club has the right amount of loft and shaft length to make it easy for most women to control. Once your swing is established, you can move confidently to master other clubs. Your basic swing will not vary: It should be the same for a Number 1 wood as it is for a Number 7 iron.

AT HOME ON THE RANGE!

If you take golf seriously, never take it for granted! The pros surely don't! You'll find them spending countless hours on the practice range working on all phases of their game.

BUILDING A STRONG LEFT ARM EXTENSION

During practice sessions, work on building a strong left arm action through the ball. Drop the right arm from the club at the top of the swing and follow through with the left arm only. This exercise will help you establish left arm and hand dominance, which is particularly helpful if you tend to have an overly assertive right hand. Note the strong left hand and arm extension in the illustration.

What to forget during practice

There are two elements which many women feel tend to hamper practice: The presence of an audience and an obsession with distance. Practice involves concentration and the discipline of mind and body. It is not playing to a gallery by hitting balls long distances. If possible, try to get off by yourself for practice sessions. Or better yet -- work with a professional golfer prior to, and during, practice.

A Note To The Left-Handed Golfer:

If you are a "leftie," and want to play golf left-handed, go ahead and do so! Do not let anyone try to talk you out of it by using the old argument: Since you have a naturally strong left hand, why not play golf right-handed and make the most of your strong left? While the advice may be well intentioned, it could also lead you into any number of problems with left and right side muscle coordination and control. At its best, golf is an unnatural game which calls for an extraordinary amount of muscle control. "Doin' what comes natrullie" for your left-side coordination is, therefore, vital if you are a left-handed golfer and intend to remain one!

It should be evident from reading this book that golf is neither a right nor a left handed game. Rather, it is a game of mind-over-body control in which *you* call the shots. Developing a smooth, rhythmical golf swing is the key to successful golf for *any* golfer! Right-handed, left-handed, or ambidextrous.

CHAPTER SIX

THE PSYCHOLOGY OF GOLF:
YOUR GOLFING MENTAL ATTITUDE
(A TALK WITH A PRO)

Someone once said that the most important distance in golf is the six inches from ear to ear. Would you agree with that?

Most definitely. No matter how good your body coordination and control are in golf, if you don't approach the game with a positive mental attitude, then this most difficult game will become almost impossible to play. "Mind over matter" is more than a mere catch phrase in golf. It is an essential prerequisite for anyone who wishes to take up the game seriously and become master of it--not letting it become master of them. Golf is a game which requires enormous concentration as the body responds to the directions from the mind. Without that total concentration on your game and on the strategies you will use during play, your golf game will go nowhere.

Where do most amateurs go wrong in their mental attitude toward golf?

Amateurs tend to be too idealistic in their approach to the game. They demand perfection. Professionals do not. The professional golfer tends to know herself and her game a lot better than her amateur counterpart. Pros put less pressure on themselves while they are on the course by *not* seeking perfection.

Amateurs always look for the shortest distance from tee to green. Invariably, they will try to achieve their goal by playing straight down the middle of the fairway. On the other hand, the pro always strives to stay away from trouble and will often choose the longer route to the hole. The amateur will go straight for the pin, as opposed to the professional who will shoot at the big part of the green and leave herself margin for error, thus placing less pressure on herself. Her muscles don't tense up as the amateur's so often do when seeking to hit that "perfect" shot. My advice to amateurs would be: Always leave yourself room for some margin of error--unless you are really on your game. Avoid shortcuts. More often than not, these can lead to trouble. Shoot for an area where you have some leeway. Don't gamble in golf unless you really know what you are doing.

Suppose you are a twice-a-week amateur golfer. You're standing on the first tee looking at a seemingly endless 500-yard hole. How will your mental attitude differ from that of a professional's?

The pro will have a game plan or strategy in mind before she approaches the first tee. She will know beforehand precisely how she should play each hole, and will play accordingly, knowing her strengths and limitations. On the other hand, the amateur will allow the scorecard to dictate what she *should* do, rather than what she *can* do on a particular hole. Again, it is so important to be realistic about your game. Not every woman can reach a par-5 hole in three shots, so why put pressure on yourself trying to do so? Rather, take an extra shot to reach the green and take the pressure off by thinking par-6, rather than par-5. Now, this is not to say that a woman should set her sights low in golf and be satisfied with a consistently mediocre performance. As in so many other sports, it is essential that we set realistic goals for ourselves and strive to reach these goals each time we play.

We all know that practice can make perfect in golf, yet why is it that many women don't like to practice their golf game?

Time is an important factor in any sport, and it is especially important to the busy wife and mother. Many women feel that they don't have the time to practice their golf game. Also, they are unwilling to spend any unnecessary money on the game and will not take lessons from a pro. Consequently, their game doesn't improve and golf becomes a source of frustration rather than satisfaction to them.

With the growing interest in women's golf, amateur women are beginning to revise and upgrade their performance expectations. Increasing numbers of amateurs are budgeting their golf time better. Rather than playing 18 holes with no practice, they will spend, say, one-half hour practicing with a pro and then play nine holes. The long-term benefits and satisfaction from playing better golf more than compensate for the time, money and effort spent on a practice range with a teaching professional. Anyone who has followed the women touring pros knows that they spend countless hours on the practice range. The seemingly effortless game you see on TV is a result of intensive and extensive practice sessions. So you see, there's no easy road to par for any of us, amateurs and professionals alike.

How do you determine your strategy for playing a course?

In her autobiography, Helen Hayes stated that she was a star before she became a good actress because only after she learned how to follow the directions of the director did she become an actress. You really don't become a good golfer until you learn to do what the course tells you to do.

When an architect designs a course, he has something definite in mind for each hole. The smart golfer will let the course and each individual hole on the course dictate what she should do. Let the hole tell you where to place the ball and how far you should hit it in order to get from tee to green with a minimum amount of trouble. Do you have to take a gamble, or can you take the safe way? Where are the trouble areas you should avoid, even although they are on the "short route" to the green? Should you hit your shots hard or hit them easier for placement? What weather conditions are influencing play on the course? Are the greens holding because they are soggy or will a head wind stop your ball as it lands on the green? These are only a few of the questions you should ask yourself to determine how the course ideally should be played. Let the course help make your decisions for you and your golfing skill help put these decisions into effect.

When we were small kids, we used to love to play in the sand. Why is it that so many women (and men) golfers are "psyched out" as soon as their ball lands in a sand trap?

The main problem lies in the amateur's reluctance to take a full swing, especially when the trap is located close to the green. Your natural reaction is to take a short swing, which frequently leads to an ineffectual shot. When you play a sand shot, think of the club hitting the sand rather than the ball. In fact, it is the momentum caused by the clubhead blasting the sand—and not the ball—which carries the ball out of the trap and gives it that sandpaper effect when it hits the green and stops dead. Again, it is very important to get to a pro and practice sand shots. That way, you will gain confidence and cut down on your score.

Is the woman golfer psychologically at an advantage in her short game?

Very definitely because she doesn't have the same underlying compulsion to muscle and "kill" the ball as she does on longer shots. Developing skill around and on the green helps take the strain off your longer game. The more shots you have in your golf game, the better the player you will become. By developing a strong short game, you can compensate for lack of distance off the tee or on the fairway. There's no question that what happens around and on the putting surface settles many golfing matches. The smart amateur will increase her chances of scoring well by working on her short game.

What are the essential differences in approach when practicing golf and when playing golf?

In practice, you are concentrating on developing a specific aspect of your game and you will work on that one area specifically until you perfect it. In playing, however, all of your mental energies should be concentrated on what strategy you are going to use on each particular hole. If you play on the same course most of the time, set your personal goals each time you play, and try to meet, and break, these goals during each succeeding game.

If you had one single piece of advice to give to the amateur woman golfer, what would it be?

Don't be so result-oriented in your game that you don't leave yourself time to work on individual aspects of your golf game. *Making a good score* is so important to so many women that often we fail to concentrate on *how to obtain* that good score. Keep in mind that golf is a game of "highs" and "lows." Both of these conditions can be potentially dangerous to the golfer who is overly prone to result-orientation. If she plays an excellent game, she becomes apprehensive as to whether she will equal her performance next time around. Conversely, if she shoots poorly, she becomes equally apprehensive about an equally poor performance during the next game. There's no question that we all have bad days, pros and amateurs alike. But the pros reaction to those "off" days is a positive one. The pro who has had a bad day will regard her poor performance as a challenge to be met. Most likely, unlike the amateur, she will head for the practice range and work on the part of her game which was giving her problems. Her problems thus become a challenge to be met and overcome.

Golf is a game of challenge. It is the challenge of you versus you. Of you versus your clubs. Of you versus the course. To meet that challenge and to overcome it is surely one of the most rewarding experiences we can have in the woman's world of golf.

NOTES

A Note About Notes

If you are a serious student of golf, and want to develop your game to its fullest potential by taking lessons with a pro, we strongly urge that you take notes after each practice session. That way, you will have a future reminder about those areas of your game which will require further practice.

Don't leave you golf game up to chance and a sometimes faulty memory — take notes!

NOTES

NOTES

NOTES

NOTES

NOTES

NOTES

NOTES

NOTES

NOTES

NOTES

NOTES

NOTES

NOTES